W9-BEV-789

A Benjamin Blog
and His Inquisitive Dog
Guide

Brazil

Anita Ganeri

Heinemann
LIBRARY

Chicago, Illinois

© 2015 Heinemann Library
an imprint of Capstone Global Library, LLC
Chicago, Illinois

All rights reserved. No part of this publication may
be reproduced or transmitted in any form or by
any means, electronic or mechanical, including
photocopying, recording, taping, or any information
storage and retrieval system, without permission in
writing from the publisher.

Edited by Dan Nunn, Helen Cox Cannons, and
Gina Kammer
Designed by Jo Hinton-Malivoire
Picture research by Ruth Blair and Hannah Taylor
Production by Helen McCreath
Originated by Capstone Global Library Ltd
Printed and bound in China by Leo Paper Group

18 17 16 15 14
10 9 8 7 6 5 4 3 2 1

Library of Congress
Cataloging-in-Publication Data
Cataloging-in-publication information is on file with
the Library of Congress.
ISBN 978-1-4109-6665-0 (hardcover)
ISBN 978-1-4109-6674-2 (paperback)
ISBN 978-1-4109-6692-6 (eBook PDF)

Acknowledgments
We would like to thank the following for permission
to reproduce photographs:

Alamy: Greg Balfour Evans, 4, Horizons WWP, 21,
imagebroker, 18, Manfred Gottschalk, cover, Paul
Springett 05, 13, Photoshot Holdings Ltd., 10, Simon
Reddy, 20; Getty Images: AFP, 17, Caterina Bernardi,
14, Diego Lezama, 25, FIFA/Alex Livesey, 22, Jeremy
Walker, 27, John W. Banagan, 6, Latincontent/Jan
Sochor, 19, Mike Theiss, 23, National Geographic,
15, Rowan Castle, 8; Science Photo Library:
PLANETOBSERVER, 9; Shutterstock: cifotart, 12,
Costas Anton Dumitrescu, 11, Mark Schwettmann
, 29, wavebreakmedia, 28; Superstock: Hemis.fr, 7,
imagebroker.net, 16, Robert Harding Picture Library,
26, Stock Connection, 24

Every effort has been made to contact copyright
holders of material reproduced in this book. Any
omissions will be rectified in subsequent printings if
notice is given to the publisher.

All the Internet addresses (URLs) given in this
book were valid at the time of going to press.
However, due to the dynamic nature of the
Internet, some addresses may have changed,
or sites may have changed or ceased to exist
since publication. While the author and publisher
regret any inconvenience this may cause readers,
no responsibility for any such changes can be
accepted by either the author or the publisher.

007017LEOF14

Some words are shown in bold, **like this**. You can find
out what they mean by looking in the glossary.

Contents

Welcome to Brazil!

Hello! My name is Benjamin Blog and this is Barko Polo, my **inquisitive** dog. (He is named after ancient ace explorer **Marco Polo**.) We have just gotten back from our latest adventure—exploring Brazil. We put this book together from some of the blog posts we wrote on the way.

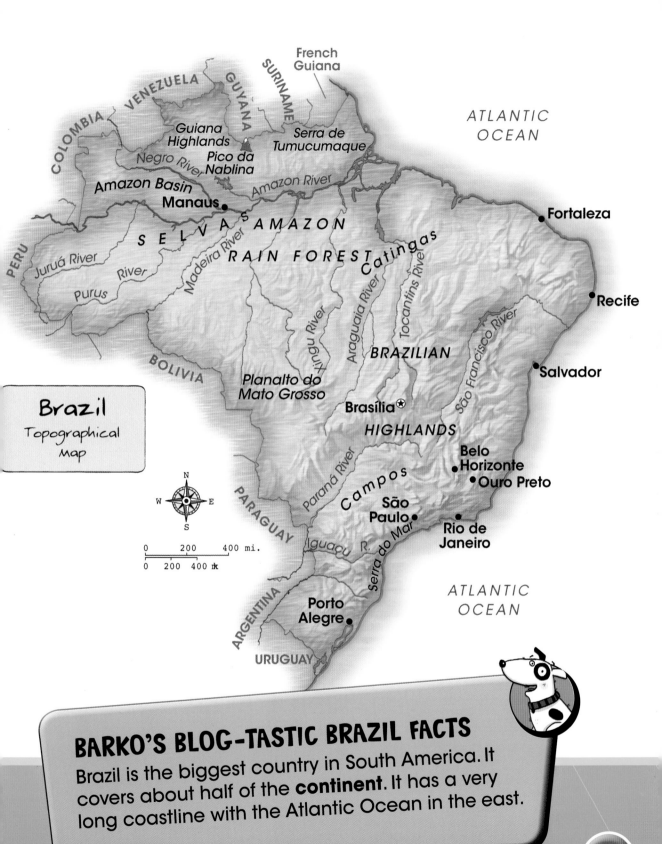

Brazil
Topographical
Map

ATLANTIC OCEAN

COLOMBIA
VENEZUELA
GUYANA
SURINAME
French Guiana

Guiana Highlands
Pico da Nablina
Negro River
Amazon Basin
Serra de Tumucumaque
Amazon River
Manaus

PERU
S E L V A S   A M A Z O N
Juruá River
River
Purus River
Madeira River
R A I N   F O R E S T
Catingas
Xingu River
Araguaia River
Tocantins River
São Francisco River

Fortaleza
Recife

BOLIVIA

Planalto do Mato Grosso
BRAZILIAN
Brasília
HIGHLANDS

Salvador

N
W   E
S

0   200   400 mi.
0   200   400 k

PARAGUAY
Paraná River
Campos
São Paulo
Serra do Mar
Iguaçu R.

Belo Horizonte
Ouro Preto
Rio de Janeiro

ARGENTINA
Porto Alegre

ATLANTIC OCEAN

URUGUAY

BARKO'S BLOG-TASTIC BRAZIL FACTS
Brazil is the biggest country in South America. It covers about half of the **continent**. It has a very long coastline with the Atlantic Ocean in the east.

Historic Places

On day one of our trip, we are in Ouro Preto, a city in the southeast of Brazil. It is famous for its amazing buildings, which were built by Portuguese settlers in the 1700s. The Portuguese arrived in Brazil in 1500 and ruled the country for more than 300 years.

BARKO'S BLOG-TASTIC BRAZIL FACTS

In 1960 the capital of Brazil moved from Rio de Janeiro to the brand-new city of Brasília. This is the National Congress Building.

Mountains, Rivers, and Rain Forests

Posted by: Ben Blog | October 21 at 2:39 p.m.

Our next stop was the Pico da Neblina in the north, where I took this snapshot. It is 9,888 feet (3,014 meters) tall, making it Brazil's highest mountain. Its name means "misty peak," and it certainly lives up to it. According to the locals, its top is almost always in the clouds.

BARKO'S BLOG-TASTIC BRAZIL FACTS

The awesome Amazon River starts in the Andes Mountains in Peru. It flows for 4,000 miles (6,437 kilometers) across Peru and Brazil and into the Atlantic Ocean.

The biggest rain forest on Earth grows along the banks of the Amazon River. It is about the same size as Australia, and I could not wait to explore it. Some local people offered to be our guides. They have lived in the rain forest for years and know it like the backs of their hands, so I will not get lost.

BARKO'S BLOG-TASTIC BRAZIL FACTS

The Amazon rain forest is home to an astonishing number of plants and animals. In fact, about one in 10 of all known **species** live there. This colorful **toucan** was easy to spot!

Big Cities

We have arrived in São Paulo, the biggest city in Brazil. See the picture I took! It is home to around 18 million people, so it is a very busy place. More than three-quarters of Brazilians live in towns and cities. Brazil's second-biggest city is Rio de Janeiro, about 248 miles (400 kilometers) up the coast.

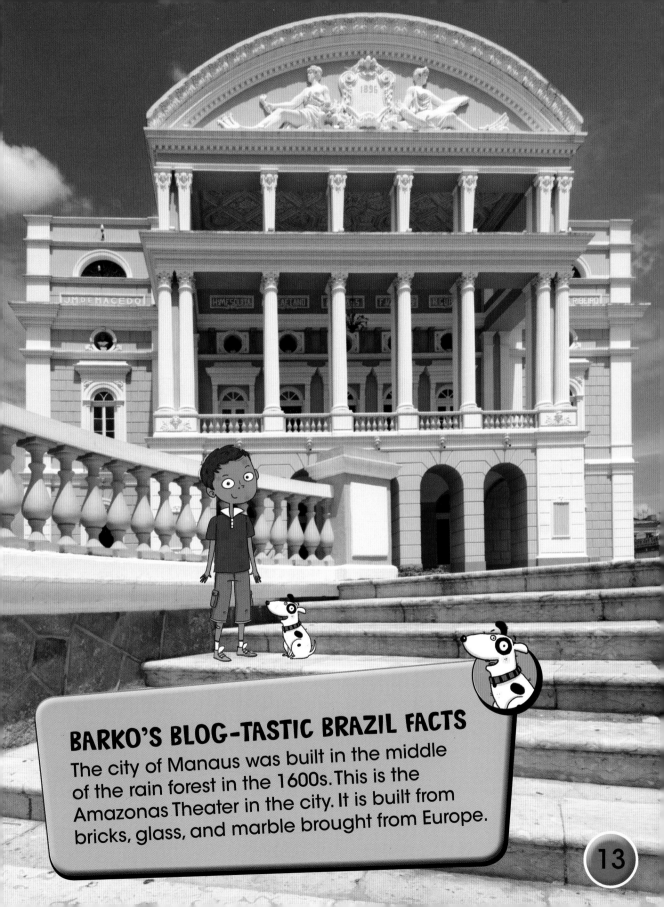

BARKO'S BLOG-TASTIC BRAZIL FACTS

The city of Manaus was built in the middle of the rain forest in the 1600s. This is the Amazonas Theater in the city. It is built from bricks, glass, and marble brought from Europe.

Bom Dia!

Posted by: Ben Blog | January 23 at 8:58 a.m.

Most people in Brazil speak Portuguese. *Bom Dia* means "good day" or "good morning." There are also many ancient South American languages. About 200 million people live in Brazil. Many of them have a mixture of South American, Portuguese, and African **ancestors**.

BARKO'S BLOG-TASTIC BRAZIL FACTS

Thousands of people, such as these Kayapo, live in the rain forest. Many still hunt animals for food and treat the forest with great care and **respect**.

In Brazil there is a big gap between the rich and the poor. Many poor people move to the cities to find work. Some end up living in **favelas** (slums), such as this one in Rio de Janeiro. The houses are made from tin or wood, and there are no toilets, running water, or electricity.

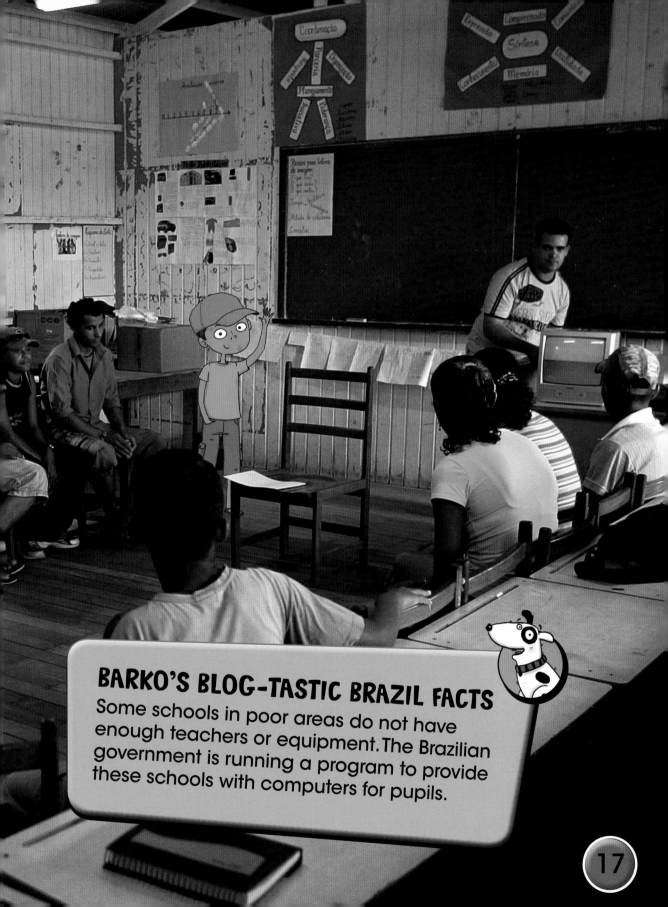

BARKO'S BLOG-TASTIC BRAZIL FACTS

Some schools in poor areas do not have enough teachers or equipment. The Brazilian government is running a program to provide these schools with computers for pupils.

We are staying in Rio because it is Carnival time—the highlight of our trip! Every year, 40 days before Easter, thousands of dancers take to the streets for a spectacular show. They are dressed in fantastic costumes that take many months to make. Is that Barko with the dancers?

BARKO'S BLOG-TASTIC BRAZIL FACTS

Most Brazilians are **Roman Catholics**, but some mix Christian and African beliefs. These people are celebrating the festival of Iemanjá, the African goddess of the sea.

A Bite to Eat

All that dancing made us hungry, so we stopped for something to eat. I picked feijoada. It is a stew made from smoked meat and beans and served with rice. It is eaten all over Brazil. Very tasty. Barko had churrasco— pieces of meat stuck on **skewers** and cooked over a barbecue.

BARKO'S BLOG-TASTIC BRAZIL FACTS

Rain forest people get all of their food from the forest itself. They hunt animals for meat, collect nuts, roots, and berries, and grow crops, such as **plantains** and **manioc**.

Soccer Crazy

Posted by: Ben Blog | March 3 at 12:10 p.m..

Staying in Rio, we are off to watch a soccer match at the Maracanã **Stadium**. The Brazilians are crazy about soccer. The national team has won the World Cup a record five times. Brazil's greatest ever soccer player, Pelé, was a member of the team for three of those victories.

BARKO'S BLOG-TASTIC BRAZIL FACTS

On the weekend, thousands of Brazilians head for the beach to surf, play beach soccer, and sunbathe. This is Copacabana Beach in Rio—one of the most famous beaches in the world.

From Mining to Coffee Making

Posted by: Ben Blog | April 18 at 9:37 a.m.

From Rio, we traveled north into the rain forest, where I took this photo of the massive Carajas mine. Here, huge trucks dig up thousands of tons of rocks that contain valuable iron. Mining is very important in Brazil, even though large areas of the rain forest are dug up to look for iron and other minerals.

BARKO'S BLOG-TASTIC BRAZIL FACTS

Brazil grows more coffee than any other country in the world. Most of it is sold in other countries. The coffee is grown on huge farms, called fazendas, such as this one in the state of Minas Gerais.

And Finally ...

It is the last day of our tour, and we stopped at the incredible Iguaçu Falls. They are between Brazil and Argentina and are 269 feet (82 meters) high and 2 miles (3 kilometers) wide. You can take a bus from the nearest town for a better view of the falls.

26

BARKO'S BLOG-TASTIC BRAZIL FACTS

This huge statue of Jesus Christ stands on top of Corcovado Mountain, overlooking Rio de Janeiro. The statue stands 98 feet (30 meters) tall, and its open arms stand for peace.

Brazil Fact File

Area: 3,287,612 square miles
(8,514,877 square kilometers)

Population: 201,009,622 (2013)

Capital city: Brasília

Other main cities: São Paulo; Rio de Janeiro

Language: Portuguese

Main religion: Christianity (Roman Catholic)

Highest mountain: Pico da Neblina
(9,888 feet/3,014 meters)

Longest river: Amazon River
(4,000 miles/6,437 kilometers)

Currency: Real

Brazil Quiz

Find out how much you know about Brazil
with our quick quiz.

1. What is the capital of Brazil?
a) Rio de Janeiro
b) Brasilia
c) São Paulo

2. Which ocean does the Amazon River flow into?
a) Atlantic Ocean
b) Pacific Ocean
c) Arctic Ocean

3. What language do Brazilians speak?
a) Spanish
b) French
c) Portuguese

4. Which is the most popular sport in Brazil?
a) soccer
b) baseball
c) tennis

5. What is this?

5. statue of Jesus Christ
4. a
3. c
2. a
1. b

Answers

Glossary

ancestor a relative from the past

continent one of seven huge areas of land on Earth

favela a poor, overcrowded part of a Brazilian city

inquisitive being interested in learning about the world

manioc a plant with potato-like root

Marco Polo an explorer who lived from about 1254 to 1324; he traveled from Italy to China

plantain a banana-like fruit, used in cooking

respect being polite and helpful to someone else

Roman Catholic a Christian who belongs to the Roman Catholic Church

skewer a long, pointed stick made from wood or metal, for cooking food

species a particular type of living thing

stadium a place where sports are played, with seats for spectators

toucan a rain forest bird with a large, colorful beak

Find Out More

Books

Barber, Nicola. *Brazil* (Changing World). Mankato, Minn.: Arcturus Pub., 2011

Kalman, Bobbie. *Spotlight on Brazil* (Spotlight on My Country). New York: Crabtree Pub., 2011

Savery, Annabel. *Brazil* (My Country). Mankato, Minn.: Smart Apple Media, 2015

Websites

kids.nationalgeographic.com/kids/places
The National Geographic website has lots of information, photos, and maps of countries around the world.

www.worldatlas.com
Packed with information about various countries, this website includes flags, time zones, facts, maps and timelines.

Index